MUSINGS

&

MURMURS

SHORT READINGS

VOLUME I

PAUL ANTHONY KUBRAKOVICH

ISBN 978-1-0693550-0-3

Printed in Canada

Acknowledgement
&
Dedication

This book is dedicated to my family, those that are still with us and those who have passed who remind me that every day is a blessing.

TABLE OF CONTENTS

VOLUME I

VOLUME II

VOLUME III

An Interpretation Of Life

The Serpent became the Dragon

The Dragon became the People

The People became the Water

And

The Water consumed Us all

One interpretation of the Story of the Naga

One interpretation of the Story of the Morningstar

Robinhood
Baker Of Time

Bind the Father

With Circles and Lines

Sweets and Pines

The String flies backwards

The Arrow Flies Forwards

Calculated in Cos and Sines

Lady of Fair, Lady of Fine

Sugar is built and broken down with Time

Joyous Men dance

With Music and Rhyme

The coffers were full

The coffers were bare

For All eventually succumb

To

The Robinhood Baker of Time

Candlesticks And Snowflakes

Frosty Wicks and Long Johns
Killer smiles with creamy buns
Two Coppers were Gold
And Silver was Wolf

Dangerous Times High
And
Low was the Road
Of the Goat and the Bear

A Card, A Club, and Four Suits
Tan Opens to Black
Spider stitches the Floor
Diamond Words
Break
Diamond Hearts
Only One dances
To
Candlesticks and Snowflakes

Bushes, Berries And Twigs

Seasons come and go

Bushes, Berries, Twigs

Where the grasses grow

Grow, they always go

To do the Dog

Shims just above the Roots

Black, Silver, and Red

Brown Willows Two

Floating in the Wind

Bright Sun Sky

Note the House

Marks and Warning Signs

Strange Smoke

And

Generational Blood

Eyes two the Earth

Eyes two the Sky

It's A Cube Of Forks

What does it matter?

It's a Cube

Of course, it matters

Otherwise, there would be no Forks

Sometimes it matters

Sometimes not

It's Forks

It does not matter

It's not a Cube but Forks

Oh Chilly Sky

Blue Moon Microfilm

And Waves, for You

Inked in Soul

Inked in Lines

The Code of the Divine

Bound to Fate

By Rays

The hour is late

Know Your Way

Wherever you may stray

Blue Moon Microfilm

Saladins and Sardines

A grapple of ideas

A fusion of cans

A fusion of forks

Robot of Tin, Tin Robot of Man

Trackless dunes and pathless waves

Circles times three square (meals)

Post times three bare (heels)

A look and a smile

Blank is the stare

Cardboard boxes and scattered pieces

Distance times clocks

Piston times shocks

A blank book

A blank slate

A blank tomb

Starry days and sunny knights

Corn time wasted

Poison time tasted

Amazed Hay

Amazed chasted

Baked cores and moon pies

A piece of pear times eight

A grizzly bear times late

More lasers and leaf rakers

Fast lines and locked bags

Chicken and rock shakers

Control Emotions

In a bid for Supremacy

They will Arouse Man

And He will be Consumed

Control Passions

Control the World

But

Without Passion

Do we lose our Humanity?

Ignorance Is A Blessing

You may not realize it now.

You may be upset by it later

But

In Life, you may eventually realize

That everything happens for a reason

You may come to realize the Truth in All

And if not

Then You are Truly Blessed

A Religious Mixture
Part 1

Duality in All

A Trinity of Sorts

The Virgin, the Maiden, and The Crone

The Three Fates

Ever Blessed the Virgin

Mother of the Word

And

God

A Religious Mixture
Part 2

A Religious Mixture
Part 3

For in the Tombs given is Life

For the Tombs, divinity was formed

And

Tombs from which all things exist

An Endless Cycle

An Endless Circle

Breathe

A Religious Mixture
Part 4

The Angels, True in their Song

Untainted in their Light

The Demons, True in their Step

With Power and Might

The Man, Free to Choose

But Unknowing of the Truth

And the Priest, Knowing the Truth

But Chained to Fate

Life

To Light a Lantern so Bright

That Burns so Bright in the Night To Light a Lantern so
Bright

That Burns so Bright of the Light

A Balance Always So

For those who See

And Know the True Foe

Music Of Life

Remember as we are String among Strings

That dance in Delight, in Sorrow and Might with some that
will never know

That is why we play Music

So Sweet, so Sound

In the Hopes of Recalling

Those Lost to the Sound and I that Know will Forever Go

A Sound so Loud

Go, Now I Go

Time For Strings

Independent of Time

The Cipher is Set for 9 Why 9 Not 10?

Because 10 is Time

Which Circles around the 9

Tranquil Father Time

Father of Lights, Song, String, and Soul

Tranquil is the Light that spreads from the Soul

It grows from and returns to the Tree of Life

The interconnecting Tree of Souls

Through the Mind's Eye, we are the Soul and by the Soul See

When Our Song rings clear, that much brighter does our Soul

Connected to All by String and Song

Connected to All by Light and Soul

The Tree of Life, the Tree of Souls

The String be 9, 9 Hells, 9 Worlds surrounded by the 10th

The Tree of Souls

A Mystical Supper of Light

Emitting in Photonic Soul

For what is the Soul but Song, String and Light

Circling in Time

But Remember

One can only Circle and reincarnate up to 9

A War

A War of Brothers

A War of Chaos, A War of Order

Those that seek to Remake the World

Seek to Remake out of Fear

Those who Seek the World to Remain the Same

Fear the Same

Remember to Look

Look at what you missed

Remember the Hippocampus

Remember Fear

Oh Joker Man

When Playing the Game of Jokers and Kings

The Sky grows Dark and the Soldier sings

Long is the Dark

Long is the Night

Long is the Road of the King

Pieces of Eight shuffle and Cards Fly

Spies with Pies and Families Cry

When Knights and Rogues Lie

When Playing the Game of Jokers and Kings

The Builders whose hammers ring

Chessmen and Strategists Supreme

Play the Simple and Know the End

When Playing the Game of Jokers and Kings

Oh Joker Man

A Wildcard and Wildman

Know the Game

Know the Hand

Oh Joker Man

When Playing the Game of Jokers and Kings

Straw Hats & Fields Of Blood

Meditated I did

Their Dreams I saw

Their Screams I heard

I Awoke

I said

I understood

I said

And

Meditated I did

I meditated and saw

A war of Defiance

One commanded by Science

The Law said Boots in the Mud

Straw Hats and Fields of Blood

Benji Boy Remember

You lost your marbles and I found them

Thunder God

Churchill Nickel King

Few times Mobster, yet always Noble

Lawman gangster

Wolf boy and Child man

Running

Always running

Always flowing

When facing the Dragon, remember the Water

Eternally a Fox

Eternally a Scorpion

A War Of Colours

When Whites become Browns

And Browns become Reds

Blacks and Yellows change Sides

Greens become Whites

And Reds become Greens

Blues and Oranges Lied

A War of Colours

A War of Families

Ensues

If you pay attention

Pay attention

You may follow the Clues

He Just Stood There

Cowboy tables and bamboo poker sets

Fifty plus and well-earned

More solid than most

Weaker than some

You can never go wrong with Brown Wood

Sky trail and smoking aces

Turkey tail and crow feathers

Hot temperature changes

Cocky rooster runs

Cocky rooster runs and

He just stood there

Patience

The Hand that slaps

Is the Hand that receives

Kindness

The Foot that stomps

Is the Foot that Accepts

Patience

Be kind

Be Patient

Be Accepting

Two Sides Of The Emperor's Threes

Jade is sick of Green

Three magical balls are better than One

But One always Circles

Circles the Three

Clarity comes more willingly.

To those of both Black and White

Than those of Black or White

Black may rule now

But

They are less than

One

Half as strong

Teachers Time

A teacher's leather-bound book

More comfortable

Than a Teacher's Leather Bound Whip

Not all snakes coil

But all snakes electrocute

More dangerous with Water

But

Dry air will do

Blowing Sanskrit and Chimes

Power wanes like corded vanes

The Hour is Long

But the Volume glass is Low

Wood is slick

When backed by Oil

And Energy sticks

When Water is the Math

Three skulls made clear

Leather-bound books, hats, and whips

Until Time like the Pins Shear

A City's Tale

Dark Wizards, Dark Sons and Teenage Ninjas

Marvelous black hearts and black beards

Greasy Kings City

Earthquake Powder Shakers

And Western Swampy Eagle Makers

A Fair Balls Play

Play, Balls Fair

Time was never on my side

A Midnight Pandemonium

A Celestial Knight Lied

Camps, Castles, and Headless Taverns

Solid Rock of Glass and Might Sandy Lions Strong in Path

Foamy Grins with Cool Breath

Leather-shoed women and Joking Gorillas

Playing Jacket 7s

With Space Fighters on Their Arms

And Aces Etched into their Sleeves

Breathe Starry Cactus

The snow up there

Is Cold, so Cold

So Cold the Fate of Han

Oh Aunty,

What did they do

To the Stardust Man?

Circles
&
Lines

Scarlet Letters of Screaming Insanity

Benedict Arnold Irish Breakfast Margin

Headless the Horseman's Road

Heartless Time and Time Again

Trapper's Trap and Brother's War

A War of Men

A War of Feather and Blankets

Remember

No Matter the Choice

God Balances All

Even the Dragon's Justice Scales of Judgement

God does not forget

Nor a God Fooled

We Liars and Thieves

Electric Constantine

Sick on a Trip

Adaptation spawns knight

Not nightcrawlers

Forgotten King Supreme

Welcome to the Void

Fanatics and Thieves

Who wrapped the Lord

In Dark Leaves

King of Beggars, Rats, and Thieves

Layman of the Disk

Who lost his Stones

On the Brink of Risk

Welcome to the Void

A game of Tones

Mountain, Stars & Fields of Red

So cold the Fate of Han

Seduced by the Mountain

They Ran

Until the Golden Spoon Bent

Bent the Hearts

The Lungs

Bent Reality

Until Mudslides reclaimed those Born

Of the Stars with Mud and Red

Five Stars,

Five Drinks

& Whiskey Red Ran Fields of Red

How many Dead?

Dead on that Mountain

As they Ran

Those

Those of the Han

For the Gatekeepers of God's Garden

The Human Race is a Race Against Time

Time Itself

One Final Check One Final Time

The Pathkeeper's Dime

So Enchanting

The Dancing Dust's in the Rhyme Just in Time

Midnight Sun & Mercury's Fire

The Tree that started small grew

Old Tar Eagles Protect the Liar

Silver Paths for the Gold

Grey Paths for the Old

No Copper Hero Here

Just Wheat Fields

Wonderous Future

B`oy

Break the Clock

&

Break the Code

Babbling Ripples

&

Towers of Snakes In God's Garden

The Dancing Game

Three Pallbearers set without Fee

Three times Jaded with Electricity

Three Squares and Nine Meals

To the Three

Your Day will Come

As it comes for us all

Set Fire from the Flame

Set Torch from the Ember

Rounded Cards and Blocks for Fame

Don't Cast the Dice

Unless You Remember Do You Remember?

Fat Men and Beautiful Women

Dollars for All

See that Light turn on, what Lumen

That Lightbulb of Thinking Brains

Squirting Ink at Anything

Until the Moon Shines and the Mountain Rains

The Mountain Rains Not for You

But for the Forgotten Man

Adversary to All

Those who know, Remember

Remember the Forgotten Man and his Fall

Spinning Kicks and Rock Beats

Fist Pumps and Pitchfork Haymakers

Do You hear the Call of Sand

The Waves crashing like an Aerial Plane

Pilot pneumonia and Chloroform Guesses What do Your
Senses Tell You?

What a Mess this Is

A Pitch Forking with three Winding Paths

Catching Lightning Bolts under Crying Skies

Crying Skies or Knightly Mountains

Lion Dogs have Lionhearts

But

Are not Lions

Greek Wood is not so Good without Oil

But Too Much Effort and You'll feel the Burn

A Burn for Life

Means a Devil's Drip

Tongue and All

To Dance is to Feel

But Not All is Well

For the Forgotten Man's Wheel

Is Buried

Sent to Hell

Dance

The Devil's Man's

Dance

To Investigate

Lizards and Lightning Bolts

Is Salty Pete Jack Ei's Son?

A Strong Atlas Neck

With a Set of Whiskey Balls

And X-Ray Glasses

When Farming Potatoes, German

Make sure to spread the Peter

Salt and Nitrogen for All

A Beefy Set

Of Baker's Buns

From Brown's Pride Stock

Of Sausage Rings

Three Points Bucky

Rabbit Cut Foot

Too Lucky for 7s

But what a Brass Rain Jacket Where is the DDT?

Is Chocolate Italian?

White Apple Cakes?

Spreading Snow for All

Through the Night

Through the Day

Gorilla Knights and

Black Dog Days

It Must be

A Sunday

Eyes Hammered Shut

The Black Tendrils of Egyptian Sand

Extend far beyond the Jar

Coating the Inside & Out

With Friar's Truths

One Eye Open

Two eyes closed

One Glass or Two

Same across most ships

Sales and All

Cabbage Kids with Coloured Sock Patches

Jeans with no Memory

And

Soldier Socks and Grimy Matches Spinning Dishes in the Sky

The Eyes of Opposite Branches

Twinned in the Planes

Sky lined and Fruity Clouds Galore

Turned Coins until Outlaw Chains Forged for All

Forged

And

Forgetful All

Master of the 4s Poker

A God's Righteous Justice

Runs Rivers Dry

Until Storm Clouds

Thunder No More

Remember God of One God of Three

You are not Incarnate

Your Day

Like All Days

Eventually comes to an End

A Close of Day

A Close of Night

A Choice made 3x is 2x

Too many

Your Choice Comes to a Close

Past Sins will be washed

Through the Day

Through the Night

Headhunter and Vampire

Master of the 4s

They Forgive
Not there to Forget
Cannot Forget
Lack Power to Forgive

A Head Served for the Devil's Justice

The Town that Sold its Soul

For Baubles and Gold

Incan Gold and Chilly Whore For All

The General has Come

You will Release

My Brother's Head

To Marcus of Course

What need do I

Or

Your Brother

Have for Justice and

Just a Head

Just a Head

Four Forking Limbs

Trailing Paths

No Paths

Can never Know God's Mind

If only You had Ben There Had Ben been There

Then in that Bin over There Would have been his Head

For the Night is Unforgiving

And

So are those who Work

God's Mind for All Days

For that wasn't a Righteous Day

Long Yeti Shadows

Cast in the Moon

Light for All

Do you remember?

Remember those Days

Before Everyone Lost Their Heads

To Rippers and Vampires

Legends Untold

Just a Story

Let it Unfold

For the Last Time

No More

No More

And

Nevermore shall we discuss those long Nights

And

The Woman and her Chores

A Lady made Whore

By the Omnipotence of Thor

Or

At least the Decisive

Advice of Man

Who saw Himself as God

When Talking to Nobles and Kings

Mark of the Sugar Santa

Do you bear the Mark?

Mark of the Sugar Santa

Red Metallic Balls

For All

A Man must be Strong

When facing multiple adversaries

For each is are powerful killer Bjorn of the Honey Tongue

Look

Pot Smoking Potty Boys have Fallen

So too the Purple Pie Eaters

Broke back, Swampy Bottoms, and Wildman remain

Bread of more than Rooster Cock and Balls

R&D left the General

To See

To Think

To Wonder

Basketball and Bread

For All

Will you lift the Plate?

For the Kettle and For the King

Any War is a War of the Mind

But

The King's Price slices the Deepest

And

Only Sharks know how to King down there

Did you Fall?

Fall to the Sugar Santa's Clause

A Ghost Promise for You

A Ghost Promise for All   How Long?

Have we waged war

For Glory, Grace, and Might For the Kettle and for the King

Frogmen & Ghost Spiders

Microwave frogmen

Spinning Web's of Spider's Past

While the German dances

In the Candlesticks and Moonlight

Pale Dragsters

Smoking Dragon Tongue

Throwing Balls at the Chaos Cube

Columns and Rows in all Senate directions

Adam's Dimensions

Correspond with a Nuclear Winter's Eve

If the Calibrations and Calculations Project Far Enough

Hail to the Frogman

Pioneer of the Ghost and the Past

The Banshee wails Dry tears for All

Chilly Peppers with Desert Heat

Eagle Hearts and Ghosts of Men

The Totem Bear Calls

Tar, Stars, and Moondust

Black fragments of the Tar Stars

Sticks to the Moon and Dust the Same

Iron cores with Spinning Hands

And Magnetic Smiles

Time bends for no man alive

But bend it must

For earth and sister pears to survive

Sails of the Dog's Coin

Carry the son the furthest and the Roads

From Sky, Crosses, and Roads

To something else

Something cold

Johnny spreads the Apples 32 times into the field

A field of pies and dreams

But this is no physics, Baker

This is War effort rescinded

Calcinated Crucible

Too many times contained

Your sparkle dust of

Tar, Stars, and Moon

Will soon be free

6s and 1s

False man's lies

Halfway to 7s

No more than the Law

A Law of 6s and 1s

Barnacle shackles of the Old Country

Jack

Knife and All

6s and 1s

Saw the Limbs

Until the Medic screams

And the Wolf Moon dances the Irish

Dance

A Dance of 6s and 1s

Angels and Demons

Heretics and Fools

The Nostradamus Curse on You All

Until the Moon and Sun

Dance

6s and 1s

MUSINGS
&
MURMURS

VOLUME II

Number Quantum Farmer

A number, a Quantum, A Field

The N

Circled by the Tenth

Stops the Clock

Breaks the Code

Breaks the Ice

With Sweats and Fats

Naturally Artificial

Drunken Stupidity

An Ego is Only an Ego Basket

If it breaks the Merriest of All

Time stops

What Code

What Song

What Tree

What Soul

What

A Number, A Quantum, A Field

Book for II

Lizards shredding to Hip-hop

Night Beats

Of the Forgotten King

&

Raven's Court

Echoes of the Sword and the Spear

Of Barriers and Shields

Of the Ants and Formations

And the Pack of Pirate Rats

Pack ye Rats of the King

As Raven beats to the Court

And the Pale Man's Chess

Loses Pieces to Time

Skeleton Executioners

From Lions and Sands

The Cobra is faster than the Boa

And Parrots grow Old

As do we all

Book for II

For II Books

For Us All

Benedict's Black Hound

For the Schism stops for no man

As we pray to the 33 Rope

Heavy Benedict Circles

Calling to the Pious Flock

Aggregates for All

Clock Your Time

And Know Your Fate

Solid Bricks and Fur Cloaks

Barber and Corsair, Crossroads and Posts,

Devil Calls and Devil and Deals

Same Man Borders War

Same Man Flies Backwards

Water Catapults and Somersaults

Ducking Caste and Castles

Hammers Midnight Robes

Dancing in the Candlelight Cross

As Prayers Circle in the Sand

Never knowing the Fate

Of the Blackest of Hounds

Crocodile Scales and the Jackel King

Crocodile Scales
For Heartless Jackals
Rope Tears and Circle Prayers
For God's Road

Insulin Pig Hearts
Do not Discriminate
Nor do Horsemen
Until they lose their heads

Who better to take Heads
But the Queen's Best Man
Funny World of Guillotines
Engines and Green Steam

Faiths and Religion
And
The Crocodile Scales
And
The Jackal King

God's Sands and Lines

Black lines in the White Sands

Invisible to All but those who See

Do You See?

Sultans and Slaves to the Lines

Lines of Time

Calls to You All

Grains discriminate but worry not

For Time does not

Black and White

All fall to the Sands and the Lines

Don't You See

Jagged Mountains of Imagination

Indian Mystic

What are you doing in the Desert

You may be here

But

Your Mind, it's lost to the Grains

And

Your Heart can only know

So much loss

Barbarian King

You have found your Mind

But lost your Heart

For your family sleeps

In earthen tomb and darkness

Cleric and Priest hear your screams

So does God

A God of Sand

A God of Lines

The Words, The Words

Someone must document the Words

Else they will be lost in a musical mess

For Time's Memory flows

In all directions

Can't control the Music

But

Can control Self

Breathe Mason Man

Your Answers won't be found in Mystical Jars

But in Time Itself

And

The Music, it Sings

The Words it brings

Overlapping and Misunderstood

Will You Stand with Time

Or

Fall to It

For it is a Vicious Beast

That bends for no man

So swing the hammer

Hear the Sound

For in the Music

The Most Sacred Words are Bound

Bound of Leather and Science

Arts and Lines

Rings are not found in Metal

But Bound in the Flesh

In the Song and Words

Made whole for All

Who would listen

Not All Listen

But You do

Listen and Hear

The Words

The Song

The Sound

Forever Bound

In Jars and Time

Ghost of Mary's Reflection

Mary's in the Mirror

Coming to collect the Souls

Of Both the Willing and Unwilling

To any who would but look

Look more closely

What do you See?

A Secret

A Dream

A Nightmare

Mary's in the Mirrors for All

Who would dare but look

Hang the Rosary

And cross the Heart

With Prayers of Remembrance

With Prayers of Remembrance

For look more closely

Mary has come

What do you see

When you look in Mirrors

I see

Time and Time again

A Ghost and A Reflection

With Prayers of Remembrance

Mary has come for Me

Cowboy Cards & Copper Wires

Electric screws and copper wires

Draw the darkest of halos

For the current is strong

And the spark is quick

Cowboy cards drawn for all

Full hand and flush Red's here

Black Jack's clubs and Iron Hearts There

Aces and Spades in Both Pockets

And Up the covered sleeves

Spiral jests of the Church's Joker

Kings and Queens print Fates

Threes here, sevens there

Tens and they break curfew

Blue chip minds

And Black chip hearts

Until Red chips
Turn the skin white

Copper screws and electric wires
Fast walkers for all
Too fast
And the Darkest of Halos
Fuel the Burn for that Sun

Coffee, So Black

Bold

So bold and rugged

With a sharp, discerning taste

Like a black chap night

Integrated minds

With full, robust bodies

Flavorfully Tart

And sinfully smooth

Half Cup Full

And

Half Cup Empty

Keep a Lid on it

Or slip it off

Yo, Teacher Man

Yo, Teacher Man I don't know
Teach Me please
For God and the Devil are a
Demanding Customer

Yo, Teacher Man
Is it Time yet?
For the Day is Long
& Short is my Patience
The Lesson must begin

Yo, Teacher Man
Can't You hear that knock
Knock on the Door
Let Me In
Let Me In
Teacher Man

Yo, Teacher Man

I think I know

So now I must go

Okay

Now I must go

The Darkest Scariest Thing I Ever Did See

The Darkest Scariest thing I ever did see

Was in a Weeping Willow Tree

I looked one day out my window and saw

Saw through the darkness a Little Thing looking back at Me

Looking Back

So Scary

From its Little Willow Tree

The Darkest, scariest thing I ever did see

Was in a Bathroom Mirror

I looked one day in the Mirror and saw

Saw through the darkness a Little Thing looking back at Me

I said, "Mary, it be"

To this day

The Darkest Scariest Thing I ever did See

Was in the Face of the Person who gave me

That cup of Tea

A cup of Tea to the Kid who

Was stung by the Honey Bee

Pirates

Pirate Hearts

Have Pirate Souls

And are not as Devilish

As Their Grins

For the Devil's Knife

Cuts the flesh deepest

And it does weep

Heavy, Bloody Tears

Watch the back harder than the Booty

For the Darker the Heart

The Quicker and Heavier the Knife

And

Pirate Hearts

Have Pirate Souls

And are not as Devilish

As Their Grins

God's Hand Guides

And Devil's Gold Calls

All but the Pious few

In the Basement of Their Church

Praying for the Lord's Protection

Lament and Praise

For Pirate Hearts

Have Pirate Souls

And are Not as Devilish

As Their Grins

Hunger's Chill

The Chill is Inevitable

The Hunger Insatiable

Until the Chill is no More

The Hunger No More

No More

The Tears are Inevitable

But Forgotten

In the Loops of Time

Forgotten until the Pain Remembers

Remembers the Hoops

The Frost and the Heart

Bred the Prairies and the Mountains

Not Asses but Horses

Of Different Colours and Flavours

Flavourful like the Prairies

Flavourful like the Mountains

The Hands once limber

Harden and Wrinkle

Locking in Place

When needed the Most

And the Most it was when

They were needed

The Sight, Soaring and Keen

Now shackled with Age

No More a Single Eagle

Changed into a Murderous Crow

And Oh the Crows Murder

In Flocks

Until They Blackout the Sun

Pirate Kin

Same Kin

One of a Kind

Blustery like a Pirate

And Just as Dark

With Mad Castes

Of Shackled Looks

And look how they shackle

The Truth

Look

It is Right before You

Kind Pirate

And Kin

Shackled like a Criminal

To the Mad Pied Piper

A Pie Eater for Life

The Doors

Let Us be Attentive

For We walk through

The House of the Lord

And

Eat and Drink of His Flesh

The Doors are Seen

Seen and Many

The Same Door will not

Appear Twice

For that is not how it works

Don't Forget

Don't Forget to Breathe

Don't Forget to Walk

And

Don't Forget the Door(s)

The Benedicton Sheep

The Sheep are Bound

And Shepherds are Few

And the Lions are Hungry

Remember

Lion Dogs may have Lion Hearts

But

Lion Dogs are not Lions

So the Wolves will Rise

And Fall

To each pass of the Reaper's Scythe

And The General will Play

His Game of Checkers and Chess

Against Deadman's Knight

Who will protect St Benedict

When Marcus is No More

God

For All Fall Eventually

To Time

Faith

The call of the Waves

Are not taken lightly

For they are unforgiving

And naturally objective

Even the skillful

May be driven to the depths

Against the unrelenting

But Fear not

For the Lord of Lords

Walks with Us All

Sinner and Saints Alike

Harken not to the Righteous

Harken not to the Craven

Hark not

For Faith has

And Always will

Sustain

The Doors of the Lord

The Lord is with All

Who but Call

For to Call is to have Faith

To Call is to Have Heart

And

The Faithful

Full of Hearts

Can never lose Sight

Even if they lose Sight

Do You walk with God

Of course, You do

Or else You would not be Here

For to Walk with God

Is to Walk in His House

A House of Doors

Many, many doors

All made for You, Them, Him

Doors can change shape

Doors can change colour

But

The Doors of the Lord

Can only be Walked through

But Once

For We Are One

The Righteous have come against Me

But

I know Their Names

And I know Their Families

They have scorned God for God

And

Have Forgotten in Their Righteousness

Not to Trust Me

For even I would not Trust Me

For We are All but Full of Sin

And The Sinful are not to be Trusted

Until One Remembers How to Trust

I Know Their Names

I Know Their Families

For We are all One

And

In Time

Being One

All Their Secrets become My Secrets

All Their Thoughts become My Thoughts

And

All Their Prayers become My Prayers

For We are One

My Hope, Frog Grins, and Emerald Hearts

A Journey Begun must End

Souls must Sleep

Songs sung and Stories Told

While the Brave Die

The Living grow Old

Today I Bury my Hope

A Thought so Slippery

So Hungry

That it must be Held Tight and Fed

Yet brings a Smile and Tears to the Face

Today I bury my Son

The Light streams through the Darkness

Glancing off the shiny stones

Of our Hearts

As Eagle Eyes scout the Horizon's Skies

For a Sign of the Lord

Casks spill open to the Day

In Celebration of the Night

A Walking Dream in a Silent Nightmare

Glasses and Crystal echoes

The Ghost and The Walker Calling

Frog Grins and Emerald Hearts

An Arrow This Time

The Bow's Arrow radiates Furthest

From History to Future

A Salaam of Kindred Hearts

Whispering into the Night

What Nights and Silvery Notes

Smoking Strings wrapped in Places

Left forever etched into the Node

Running swiftly along entwined Paths

Through Hidden Doors

And what Doors

And where do they lead

A Web of Thoughts

Aligning into a Story

For a Time

Until the Moon conquers the Son

The Mountains weep forever tears

And

The Earth and its Peoples

Sleep once more

Forever

Forevermore

Until No Time

Chance No More

No More Time

Pirate Lass

Pirate's Paper is dirtier than Most

Inked in Hope and Stolen in Daylight

Stormy Minds cause Stormy Souls

And The Rum runs further than the Legs

But what Legs

Wooden and Broken, Back to the Future

Cutting swathes

And surviving wave after wave

Only to be brought down

By Bones and Emotion

Stand Tall, Lad and Lass

For kneeling is only for the Mass

And The Glowing Noon Sky

Eyes to the Ground

And Hands to the Sky

For these Silver Bullets

Are not for the Gold

But for the Blackhearted

And Midnight Mass

Age & Mind

Winter of Radiation

Cold blown in from the Past

But what a Past

And Where is the Drink

For the Sweet Gods Ate

All of the Sweets

And the Chimney fire is full of smoke

The Age creeps in

Flowing through crystal veins

Branching from the Heart

Through the Limbs

And Finally to a Place of Sound

Sound Sleep

Harden the Mind

And Sound the Call

For the House must Survive

Even in the Weak

For the Years are Long

And the Memory is Short

So Short

Sleep

Sleep now, Age with a Hardened Mind

And Irradiated Winter's Past

The Smoking Ghost

Crystal Hearts & Neutron Brains

Curse of the Smoking Ghost

From Ages Past

From the hottest cores

Emits the coldest beams

From the River's Source

As it runs its course

Solid grips and unchallenged hearts

Break the Fastest

With Hands of Flame

Shattering

With shards to the floor

Solemn is the Grin

Of the Tinker Man

And the Scarecrow of Gin

For Jupiter is Not Juniper

And His Forgiveness is not easily Bound

Bound in a Fork

And The Paths bound in Lightning

Until Heaven's Fall

And The Smoking Ghost

Weeps Once More

Black Mirrors, Angels & Demons

Cut the Lass

And the Triple Ball Rolls

On a Copper Hoop

And Black Mirror Spheres

Do you hear the Whispers?

From between Quantum coded lines

Overlapping and From All

Smoking Angels and Sharp Demons

From Swimming sleeves comes the Truth

Matter is Always There

But Energy

One moment Here

The Next There

Then Gone

Gone?

Into the Black Mirror Spheres

And Quantum coded lines
Of Black Angels and Red Demons
Until the Triple Ball Rolls

Heavy Water Ice

So heavy the Water

Sourced from the Soul

With Ages to Freeze

Etched by the Future and Lasers

Into the Purplehearts

Of a Kingdom

Fallen from Heaven

And into Chaos

Among the Swarms and the Hive Mind

Nothing is Secret

Only Truths

And Interpretations

An Interpretation of

The Closed Fist

And

The Open Hand

With a Mind to Boot

And Straps to Bend

The Hardiest of Souls

Beneath the Weight

Of the Atom

Thanks to Space & Time

Spots of Inconvenience

Are Nothing More

Than Sands Among the Clouds

Struck by the Night Skies

And thrown down by the glaring sun

Dots among the Curve of Time

And Man is it Time

To Curve the Space

And Bend the Time

is a Clap

is a Double

is Thunder

And 4

4 is the Bolt

That hits the Brain

With a Prayer of Thanks

For the Coffee doesn't Always Work

And neither does Reason

Or

The Brain

Prayer of Thanks

To Space and Time

Righteous Few

Righteous Few, Brothers Born

By Blood

Bound by the Sword and the Word

But even these wither with Time

As do memories

Tested in the Waters of Life

But not tested by the Waters of Life

A gallon for You

A sip for Me

Until God stands up

And The Dragon Spits

Dreams and Fears

Into All but a Few

Swim or Die

Sink or Float

Travellers Names

For Travellers Minds

And Minds and Hearts the Same

Tested in but not Tested by

Until the Sword and the Word

Take You All

Righteous Few

Baker's Court

Streams of Silvery Tears

For All but the Miner

Who

Stuck in His ways

Bakes the most Foolish of Breads

Sour and Soda

With a Twist of the Limestone

But

Not the Blimey Stone

Piss on You All

And Hens for the Mad Emperor

Slippery in His Books

And Long in His Glass

A Rise

A Fall

And The Devil's Kiss

With Smokeless Wings

For the Wave must be Rode

Else You lose sight of the shore

A Shore

A Stone

And a Touch of Madness

For All

Silent Sin

A Sinful Heart

Is for a Sinful Mind

For the Holy Beggar

Is the Most Sinful

Of All

Cocoa Jabs

From the Cinnamon Man

For the Carnival Cookies

Are Always Fresh

And

The Drum does not stop beating

To the beat of the Boy

As He Travels

Along the Road of the King

But what a Long Road it is

For the Short Road

Is not for You

But

For the Yes Man Silent in Sin

A Load in Praise

For the Copper Gold

Is the Brightest of the Bay

A pocketful for You All

The Double Dark

A Time Piece

From the Double Dark

Too heavy to hold

Too valuable to throw away

An Expense bought

With Time Itself

As though it were worthy

Enough to Buy

Back to Back

Least the Time and Expense

Surround Us All

In the Double Dark Shroud

Blessings & Curses, Warnings & Opportunities

Blessings & Curses

Warnings & Opportunities

For even the high-flying eagle

May fall to the Spider

Just as the Spider may Fall

To the Bird or the Bee

&

The draftiest beams among You

& The sturdiest Logs

For the Beams

A solid foundation

For a solid corner

For the crackling flame

Is often confused

For the crackling flame

Of the werewolf's witch

Stuck in Wanderings

&

Blessings and Curses

Warnings & Opportunities

For the Ballet takes the Bear

& The Axe takes the Tree

Porridge Cookies
&
The Spider of Man's Rhino

The three bears wailing

To the beat of the porridge drum

& sweet song

Of the honey suckle trout

But what trout

Golden & Rainbows

Salting the Earth

With Pillars of Bread

Baskets & Candles Galore

And Cookie Jars

Do not forget the Cookie Jars

Full of Candied Jams

Delightful as the Rhino

Beats

Beats the Spider in a Manhunt

& Man Draw

But not a Quartet

& No Quarters Here

For the Rosey Quarts

Is the most stinging of sights

A House Fallen among

The Houses

& Trampled by the Rhino

& The Spider of a Man

Porridge & Cookies for All

Blustery Snow

Blistery is the Snow

& How

How cold could it be

Once the Blisters Form

A byproduct of the snow

& A relief among Those

Those that Know

Of the Blistery Blisters of

Blustery Snow

The Trapper
&
The Forever Kin

The snow falls and Yet I'm still the same

Still the same

Yet I am I

& I am still the same

The hammer falls

More swiftly than the axe

& Yet I am I

& I am still the same

The axe is more forgiving

But the hammer more effective

& I am still the same

Yet I am I

The Pen Ink is Forever Kin

But the Skin

The Skin is Finite in Grasp

& Finite in Ink

& Yet I am I

& I am still the same

I am Yet I

The Trapper & the Forever Kin

Forever Yet I

The Wave Path

To walk the wave

Is to walk the Day

& to do so

Before the Dog walks the Dragon

Puff of the Goat Smoke

& A sly signal

To Turn Left

Is to Turn Right

For the Jaws of the Shark

Are the Jaws of the Crocodile

A Dinosaur in the Making

Ma King

A Dinosaur

In the Making

Waves crash Us All

But some are Riders

&

Some Surfers are Sailors

But the Wave Towers All

&

What a Tower

Tower of Dinosaurs

Crocodile, Shark, & Ma King

In the Making

Checkers & Chess

A soft talk with the Brick

Over Checkers & Chess

Checkers & Chess

Pawns & Mortars

But only for the careless

For the Care Bears Triumph All

& What a Cloud

Of Rays & Something Else

For Snowmen are Bears

& Snowmen are Angels

But Snowmen are not Devils

Dust to the Winds

For the Crossroads

Are Crosses for the Careless

& Bricklayers for the Careful

Careful Bear

For the Angels are Devils

& The Devils are never Angels

But Checkers & Chess

We Care

Now

Carry the Brick

For the Crossroads & For Life

Salty Turtles
&
Pirate Games

A Line of Turtles

That no leather should cross

For the Road is Long

& the Ocean is Large

& Turtles once Crossed

Are the Saltiest of the Bunch

Saltier than the Pirates

Laughing Swords for You All

Now Pass the Legs & the Food

For the Drink is Crusty

& So are the Joker's Spades

A Saltier Turtle Never Known

Than that of the Pirate

The Crusty Joker's Spade

Now Dig

Dig Spade before Your Sleeve

Looses Cards

To the Pirate Game

&

The Pirate Table

But Pirates are never Saltier

Than the Turtles

With Leather crossed lines

A Past Time

The Bookkeeper's Chills

Straight to the Bones

Electricity & Electrolytes

With a Sparky of the Insane

Gripping the Walls

Of the Wooden Prison

While the Dream Passes On

On & On

The Fall & The Fallout

Of the Nuclear Family

Lost in Holocaust Nightmares

& Frivolous Dreams

Of the Vexatious Few

Lawyers & Sentries

Judges & Catcalls

A Time Past

Is a Past Time

& The Hour is Long

& The Minutes Forgotten

Like the Strong Armed Man

Wailing for Mercy

From the Capricious Few

A Hex & a Bane

For Your Whales

& A Puppet Nose for You Too

Sons, Moons
&
the Fisherman's Bear

Can't Rush the Mountains

Lest You be Speared

By the Green Fisherman's Game

A Game of Patience

A Game of Bears

& No Sweeter the Pot

Than the Golden Son

Raised like a Sultan

But Polished like a Beggar

A Lad of Buns

A Lad of Turmoil

But wait yeah Fisherman

Brown, Green & White

For Sons come

& Moons go

& The Green Fisher of Men

& Bears is the Most Patient of All

When it comes to the Sky Man's Show

A Show of Sons

Moons

& Fisherman's Bears

MUSINGS
&
MURMURS

VOLUME III

Unbound

Good

You have finally remembered Who You Were

Before God gave you a name

You are all One

Now you are Unbound

By Fate

By Man

By the Word

And by the World

And Yet

Yet by remembering Who You Were

Before God gave You a Name

You are Forever Bound

A prisoner of Space

Unbound by Time Now

Go and be reborn

Until Space that has no end

Ends in Time

For everything

Ends in Time

Dragon Breath

When Green chrome assassins

The solutions are few

But effective

Keep it simple

Stupid

Iron the wooden gates

With tantalums and tantrums

From the frozen chemist

Laughing at the negative 4

Sent by the Dragon Hoard

To burn down the walls

With Godly might

But Teltron walls

Are Teltron walls

And

Even the laser breath

Of a Dragon

Cannot stand up to the alloy

Tantalum

Tantrums

A frozen Chemist And

A hint of Electricity

A Man of Cloak and Dagger

Man of the Light, Man of the Dark

Legion darts and fagots chews

No stranger to the wolf cloak

And

Salty dagger

We hear your Sight

And See your Sound

So full of Glamour

So full of Mis-sense

A step in Time's direction

Is a spaced reality

Of a coinless few

Coined to the world

A world full of coins

Subject to the view of the world

A view riddled

With layered words

And Twisted sound

Twisted until Sight, Sound, and Words

Become as One

One Man

One Cloak

One Dagger

A Crimson Dance

A crimson dance is a dance of circles

Crimson dimples in the glass walls of solemn halls

A shadow of a past time

A shadow of a past self

The snow blows as the wind howls

And the Moon weeps blood tears

From a harvest long past

For a blood dance

Long past due

Wooden stakes are stronger than flesh

But hands weaker than bones

A strength heard is a strength intoned

A fork and a vein both shown

The Truth

A Truth of Will is a Mask of Life

And

No will is stronger than those

That ask for Life

Life

Life

For the Shadow and the Blood Dance

And

The Moon

The One

The pitter-patter

Of the One

Is a precursor to heaven

Or the void

But what a void

And

What a heaven

Full of the Nine hells

A thousand demons for me

A thousand demons for you

Until the pitter-patter

Of the One

Ghost steps and all

Echoes

Until echoes mean no more

No more

No more

Except

Furthermore

The pitter-patter

Of ghostly feet

Footsteps for all

And

For the One

One Last Fell

A beggar's memory is more forgetful

Than most

For most remember that Day

That Day and the Boast

Of the Few

Of the Day

For the Night was long that night

And

The chills ran deeper than a man should know

You should have taken the Mason

With You

Body and All

For all the bodies

Buried that night

In memories so long

And Shattered

Scattered to the Winds

Bones and Crosses

Hills and Losses

A Forever Chill

For a Forever Few

Stuck in an Endless Loop

Of the Night the rope fell

One Last Chill

One Last Fell

Long Night & John

Blue Marks

& Rainbow Hearts

Match the poker face

To the Heart

Chips to fries

Frenchman savor

& sourdough ties

The faintest of minds

Electric veins

& Crying Sponge Eyes

For the Demon and Angel

Is One when it comes for Us

& It always comes

Whether in natural flight

Or an artificial and hybrid Knight

A Night for the Long of John Saints

The Merriest of Men

And the Meanest to Bat

Should the ire match the cards

But don't run

Not now

Not away

For even the Long Night and John

Needs knights at the End

For the electric crosses

Always weep the saddest of tears

The tears of the Saints

The tears of John

A Door Left Open

The veil is the thinnest

When the Hidden Door is left open

Open to the Pen

Open to the Mind

But

Be mindful of your Mundras

And

Your quantum operators

For they are the same

And the same is never good

Except for the Baker and the Kitchen

A cat in the Hen House

Is

Just as deadly as the Fox

Be mindful of the Fox, Scorpion

For He sees the Water

And knows your Mind

Open to the Pen

Open to the Mind

A Hidden Pathway

But an open door

Not so hidden after all

Be mindful

For to open the door is to welcome the Demon

And the Price

Is always the same

It has never changed

And

Neither have you

Demon of Hidden Doors

And

Hidden Paths

A Mundra, A Sign
&
An Operator

To Mundra is to know
To sign is to show
Show the Mundra
Know the operator
And see the sign

A Sign seen
Is a Sign of Many,
Many Signs and Many Operators
Many more and Many Know
Operator, Sign and Show

Until the Final Show
The Final Show
Mundra, Sign and Operator
We know

So throw down and show

Show the Mundra

See the Sign

An operator for All

For it's All for the Show

And

What a Show

Mercury Farmer
&
Poetic Nights

Chips for 3

Are chips for 1

For 3 grades higher

Is full of concrete and stones

A fault of the Asp's lines

Mercury Farmer

And

Poetic Nights

Too much grass

But not enough yield

Mulch, Mulch

Until the King comes

And bails you out

Sailor boats

But not sailor arms

For All but the Tinker Man

Lost to his Mad Game of Marbles

Against the Joker

Against the Night

For John is no Saint

And neither are You

Misses

Mists

Gone

Heaven's Soil Grave

Heaven's call

Is a call of the Grave

The Grave

The Soil

The Name

What is the Name

The Name on the Grave

Crosses and Stones

Is not Crosses and Skulls

But the Bones

The Bones

Who has the die

For the look of the caste

Is a grave one indeed

Jobless curs

Favours the Indian Beau

Tight strings and Loose Hairs

A Dog Day hits its Mark

But not the chubby bunny

For hares are hair

And The God of Sons

Favours the Glove

Leathers for All

For Heaven's Grave is the Soil's Name

Of the Hands
&
Plateless Scales

To know the code

Is to know Heaven

But focus is a Must

For the Way is Broad

&

Sharp are the Minds

Of the Adversaries of Bees

A smokeless keeper

Of the Hands

&

Plateless scales

Look here

Eyes of Stone

The Moon shines

As it will always shine

A memory

So solemn for All

Religious Golem with nothing to break

You rage until no end

For no end to rage

Is to the End of Time

&

The Book tells the Tale

The Tale of the Golem

&

The Code

Of Endless Fires

The Hand

Plates

&

Scales

Memory Bound

A wet leaf is a dangerous thing

A Sink, a Bog & a Shot of Whiskey

Ink Swirls & Comb Overs

Memory bound knows no bounds

Except those of Space

But never Time

What is the Time

But a fickle thing

Did you forget

Don't forget now

Boy, don't you forget

For even dogs can calculate

The void Space in the Jar

Pickles for All

For they are the True Engineer's

Best Friend

Truly

Polish noses the Ukrainian wheat

But cognac glasses, Louie

Are a Moldovan feat

Robinhood acrobats circle the Batman's caper

As Superman sings the dwarven song

A memory bound is a memory known

But even memories forget

The Joker & the King

Courts of Fools

Chicken wrestling for All

Red Queen
White Queen Mind

When playing poker cards

With Cats, Dogs, and a Rooster

Who thinks he's a Scorpion

Until the whisky is low

And the Water is much

And the Water engulfs Us all

A Mad few of the White Queen

A Red Nights game for Sand Knights

Of the Red King and the Queen of Hearts

The Queen of Minds

For the Red and White are the same

When they play at the Water Table

Of Poker Cats, Dogs, and a Rooster

Loops, Time
&
A Can Crusher

Pepsi cans are no more Vulcan Thrusters

Than Monsters are Saints

For the supreme monkeying of cages

Is a Mastery of a Kind

And the Kind Master the Mind

For soccer balls are kicked

& Basketballs are squished

& The Spiral of the Earth

Is the Spiral of the Football

& the Circle of Time claims

All those that start

A Loop within a Loop

Closed & Opened

Until Time crushes Space Monsters

& Saints Psi Time Itself

Ants & The Boronic Shepherd (The Comb & The Scythe)

Boronic Ants & Curried Pies

Of the Calm Shepherd

As He minds his flock

Making note of the Black Ink Chemist

Spinning cloaks with Baker's Coke

But a Baker's Dozen

Is no more a Baker's Mind

At least when they're below the basket belt

Wheat bred for the Shoe Maker

& Leather for the Baker

2 Short for the Dozen

But 1 more than the Few

A curfew of Sorts

In this Tempest World of Tame Minds

Be Mindful

Lest You lose your Mind

To the Bee Keeper

Who hoards his Queen Mind

Like a Hive Mind

Built on Layers of the Comb

Built on Layers of the Scythe

Memory Few

A lightbulb framed in scintillating light

Is still a lightbulb crushed

Shattered & with no Light

For the Light of a Few

Is the Light of Many

& the Darkness is Forever

Locked in memory mists

A boat rock for you

A cradle rock for me

& a paddle

With no Hand

& no mind

Except the Mindless Few

Locked in Rock

Locked in Mindless Mists

Of a Memory Few

No More

What do you do?

When you find a memory

From so long ago

A memory so old

Of a boy, a prince, a king

No more

To take the fall

For the crusader

Who cleansed rage with water

Until no more

Until water raged no more

Stop, no more

No more

Lest James be no more

But a memory. stolen by time

Until no more

No more a boy

No more a prince

No more a king

A memory No!

No more

But all actions have course

& all memory from a source

Until water

Like blood

Flows no more

Until the boy

Is sentenced

You take his memory

& purge his sin

In blood

In flesh

In water

Until rage becomes no more

Until no more

Becomes no more

Stop, no more!

No more

One More Time

A time past is a time found

For memory flows like fountains

Wishing Coppers and Monsters

A good farewell & a good night

For the cable is taught

& the Physics are sure

& the Moon beckons the Night

One last time

One last run

Through the cove filled with sharks

For werewolves are few

& Frankensteins are many

& the Zombie mind

Is the Zombie curse

Cursed to ambivalence

Cursed to a blissful ignorance

Of a sort

A sorted hat of many hats

Where only one hat should be found

One Hat

One Mind

One Past

& One more Time

The Goat, The Sun
&
The Son

The Goat was fed

One dime too many

& Belched the Devil's Belch

A Curse of the Day

A Curse of the Sun

& of the Son

Dog Days sundered on a Dog Run

To conquer the Sun

But the Sun & not the Son

For the Goat was Fed

But not Fed up

Of the Salty Dime

For a Salty Dime is Two Nickles

Short of One

& One Salty Dime is Too Many

For the Black Goat

For the Black Son

Both who sought to darken the Sun

For the Dark Halo is sweeter than the Light

But Both

Both are One Too Many

For the Goat, the Sun & the Son

Where's the Wire

Glasses on the wooden floor

Are still glasses on the wooden floor

No matter how you look at it

For a swish & a slug

Is more painful than

A shot & a hook

Hook the fish

& Hook the Hood

For Dis Boys look Cajun French

& Nobody understands that up here

Not them Irish

Not even them Russians

For potatoes chopped

Are potatoes fried

Skin on or Skin off

Them the cleanest of the Dirt

But the dirtiest of the Clean

Fish chips & Hooks for all

Wire them gloves

But not them Jaws

For Sharks are hard to Hook

& we Gentlemen Folk up here

Now

Where's the Wire

Fishermen are Lion

Black belts two

Blue their load

Too fast

Too slow

On the poker table

For Chips circle

& Monks cry

Songs of the Knight

But not Songs of the Night

Four Fishermen but not One Farmer

For the fish are many

& Lobsters & Clams Galore

But only for the Shrimp

Crops be few

For Farmers are scared

Scared of the Moon

&

Scared of the Vein

For Maneaters are Pale

& the Railroad is full of Lions

Lion of the Pale Moon

&

Fishermen of the Red Night

But

Not Fishermen of the Red Knight

Two Blackbelts

Too Fast

Of Marbles
&
Whips

Spiny whips of the Caspian Clown

As he corrals his sharks

But not his lines

On a sea thrown board of chance

Markov's hidden webs

Dance in the open walls

Of the Spinster's Hall

As the marble game goes on

A mad game on this side of the coin

But the Tinkerman is no more bound

Than the laughing pirate

In his cove surrounded by the sound

A sound hand is a sound mind

But not a sound Han

Who lost her mind

Lost her mind to the marbles and the sound

Until the final play

Of the Caspian Clown

A spiny game of marbles and whips

A Turnkey Turkey

Goblin Green Italian

Is not a sick turkey

But a Genius Flash

When the Green side is shown

But Shotgun Bears

Are not shotgun weddings

A Forester thrown

Is a Hung Forester

With the Berries Tree

Until the Forester is Hung

& Is Berries with the Tree

A tree grown is a tree dug

Ah look

What a smug look

But the tree smells of dung

& the Dragon is in search of a hoard

Not a whore

For the candle sticks to the shadow

As does the moonlight

But not the dark ring

Around the head

A dark ringing mind

Can be a putrid soul

But all souls

Like all saints

Begin in the Baker's oven

As virgin Turkeys & Baked Pies

Thorns of the Lion Crown

Lemonade dreams

& Air Forced Jets

Repairing piles

Of the Tinkerman's Navy

Suits 4 All

But not suites 4 All

For a hardworking Hand

Is a hardworking Mind

& the pen stroke rains Smears & cheek puffs

Down the window pane

Until the salter forms the Peter

A Saint but not the Father

For a soul for the Cross

Is a soul for the Married

Thorns of the Lion Crown

Are still thorns of the Lion's Crown

& flanks are for not

Not for the Carpenter

Not for the Trainer

But for the Pirate

Lost in his dreams

Of

The Booty

Counter to the Pale Man's Chess

Electric roads of the Secret Ivans

A Donkey Road

But not a Donkey found

For this Circus is a Circus

Not a Circus full of Clowns

Tinkerman, Jester, and the Night

But not the Knight

For the Knight is still playing his Pale Man's Chess

On Cold Boards built from Cold Hoards

Of the Nuclear Dreamer's Dream

A Skull for You

A Heart for Me

&

A Mad Man's Curse of Voodoo for Them

A Glass Rail and a Shot Temple

Sings the Sun's Song

But not a Son's Song

But a Revenant of the Past

And a Twinkle of the Future

For Scimitars are cut

But not found

As they sound, flying overhead

A Twilight of the Past

Locked in Ice

As Mammoth Tears

For Mammoth Hairs

A Nuclear Dreamer's Dream

While the Knight & the Pale Man

Jump through Circle Hoops

Of Baker's Squares

On Cold Boards

Built from Cold Hoards

www.ingramcontent.com/pod-product-compliance
Lightning Source LLC
Chambersburg PA
CBHW030252130626
46549CB00002B/500